The Wonders of Her Waves

Neira Ibrahimovic

LETTER FROM THE AUTHOR

Thank you for being here. Thank you for choosing to open your heart to my spirit. Thank you for taking this journey with me as I discover my truest expression. Life has been opening so many portals for me. About four years ago, when I had begun college and was on the search to find myself, I felt a deep calling from within. As I learned about the world through a spiritual lens, I found my place as a Light Leader in this universal path towards raising our consciousness. I started by transforming the way I perceive life, as being alive is in itself an overlooked miracle. As I found the beauty in everything around me, I also found more and more of the beauty within myself. Upon connecting with Nature and surrounding myself with people who uplifted me, I slowly released any fears of judgment. I became more confident to share my thoughts with the world, and this urge to share naturally unraveled into a collection of poems.

That brings us to where we are now. I have published my very first book, something that I have been manifesting since I began my spiritual awakening. This book is more than just a collection of poems… It is a story of a woman who discovers herself through her voice and falls in tune with life as she shares her expression. By being here, you are a part of my story.

I love you, I thank you, and I honor you.

From one soul to another,
Neira

CONTENTS

Lyrics of Love 7

Nature's Womb 31

Wild Feminine 43

Free Spirits 59

Taste Your Tears 75

Divine Union 117

Light Leaders 153

To Be Happy 163

~~~~~~~~~~~~**Lyrics of Love**~~~~~~~~~~~~~

when she whispered songs of sadness to her shielded
heart, the world listened closely. words of self-doubt
transformed as the Universe lit her path…

a shooting star, a painted sky, a ribbon of color

she found the love of the Universe all around her. and
upon deeper searching, she found the love of the
Universe within herself.

all the grays turned to vibrant color. her nights turned
to days. her whispers turned to tunes.

and when she hummed lyrics of love to her new open
heart, the world sang along to her melodies

~~~~~~~~~~~~~~~~~~~~~~~~~~~~~~~~~

You Are Enough

looking for love, my dear?
need not look far
all the love you seek breathes
through the spirit you are

To My Body

To my body:
Thank you

Thank you for giving my mind and spirit a vessel
through which I experience this beautiful Earth
Thank you for mapping together my pieces so I could
be birthed
Thank you for building a shelter for me that I could
always come home to
Thank you for adapting so effortlessly to the shapes
and sizes my spirit fills

Thank you for loving me so fully
Even at times when I didn't know how to love you

To my body
I recognize all you do for me
Every moment, you are pumping blood through me
so my portal to life could stay open
You are absorbing the nutrients that nourish me
Filling me with the air that allows me to breathe
Every moment, you are using your strength to fuel
mine — even for the simplest things
Like the way my hand is moving now to write to you
The way my chest is rising to take in the breath that
you have cleaned for me
The way my eyelids close in silent shutters so I could
open my eyes to see

It is a miracle that I am alive
To think of all you put into keeping me alive for this
moment

For every moment

To my body
I love the way you move and curve
I love the way you fold over like gentle waves on my
skin's horizon
I love the way you flap like wings on the underside of
my arms

The beauty in you exists in the different forms you
take
Each unique and new

The way leaves change colors in the fall
The way butterflies change sizes as they emerge
The way hillsides erode and take on new shapes....

Your different forms are a facet of Nature
And Nature holds the space for you to explore every
form

So from the times I didn't know how to love you
The times I thought your shapes and curves were
limited to what others said they should be
The times I felt your wings and labeled them lesser
than...

I have learned

I have learned that you are an artist
The oceans you form on my skin are the paintings
you've designed
The groves you've signed under my eyes are the
forests you've planted

The creases you've put on my thighs are the pieces of clay you've molded

You are an artist
And I love what you've created

To my body:
Thank you

What is Love?

Love is not a state of emotion
Love is a state of being
Love is not what I feel
Love is who I am

You're Beautiful

you're beautiful

not because you have blue eyes
and all the singers want blue eyes
not because you have long hair
and all the pictures flash long hair
not because you have small thighs
and all the models flaunt small thighs
not because you have clear skin
and all the ads show off clear skin

you're beautiful

because you have a vibrant laugh
which we don't hear in every song
because you have a gentle soul
which pictures cannot string along
because you're strong and powerful
which isn't shown on runway walks
because you stand for your beliefs
which ads leave out of all their talks

you're beautiful

not because you check some box
of what society deems as true
you're beautiful simply for the way
you show up in this world as *you*

Framing Beauty

You will never be able to witness yourself in your full
beauty

You've only ever seen yourself in mirrors and glass
doors
You've only ever seen yourself in reflections of
windows and small screens
If you take something that fills up space
And shrink it down to fit two dimensions
You miss out on all the beauty that comes with a full,
radiant being

You see, the pictures you use to define your worth are
deceiving

A picture cannot possibly capture the glow of your
skin in the light of the moon or the color of your eyes
in the glare of the sun

A picture cannot possibly capture the flow of your
dress as you walk through the wind or the curl of
your hairs that bounce out from your bun

A picture cannot possibly capture the crinkle in your
nose when you giggle and smile or the rise of your
shoulders before you exhale a sigh

A picture cannot possibly capture the joy of your
laugh as you throw your head back or the dimples
that form on your cheek when you're shy

Why do we trust pictures of us to create our
perceptions of how we appear
When pictures remove the dimension of *life* that is
needed to make our perceptions more clear?
A living person cannot flatten down into a phone
screen or glass door
Your reflection cannot possibly capture how beautiful
you are in full form

We will never be able to witness ourselves in our full
beauty...

So next time we feel like comparing our reflections to
real life embodiments of each other
Let's imagine instead how beautiful we are when
admiring ourselves from the eyes of another

Mirror Mirror on the Wall

Mirror mirror on the wall
I grew up thinking you knew it all
I trusted you to unveil my truth
That's what the stories taught us to do
So I placed my worth in what you showed
And my insecurities began to grow
The whispers of the girls at school
Said "pretty" came with many rules
I looked at you with bitter eyes
Pinched my waist and pressed my thighs
My mind was clouded by the view
I lost myself when finding you

My heart aches for the little girl
Who thought her mirror showed the world
From reading all the princess books
She learned her value came from looks
But now I've grown and I've realized
Beauty lies beyond the eyes
I find my purpose in my heart
In my message and my art

Mirror mirror on the wall
You surely cannot know it all
If you don't show me what's inside
Then I don't trust you as my guide
I love the kindness that I share
I love the way I truly care
I love the courage that I hold
I love the way I'm strong and bold
I love the energy I give
I love the way I choose to live

I love my faith in the divine
I love the way I feel aligned
When I look at who I am
I am proud of where I stand
The Love I now so deeply feel
Expands beyond what you reveal

Mirror mirror on the wall
Who's the fairest, after all?

Don't Call Me Pretty

don't call me pretty
i've heard it too many times before
behind the layers of my skin
there exists so much more
call me kind
call me caring
for always leading with my heart
call me gifted
call me creative
for expressing my soul's love through art
call me intelligent
call me sharp
for thinking through the toughest times
call me courageous
call me strong
for persisting when there was no light
call me loyal
call me honest
for abiding firmly by my word
call me joyful
call me vibrant
for laughing more to brighten the world
i'll say it again
don't call me pretty
my appearance isn't all of me
i hope next time you can find
who i am beyond what eyes can see

Kiss Your Wings

to the girl who
clipped her wings
so she could fit
into the box
of *perfect*...

it is time
to kiss your wings
& break free

Life's Signature

Let the calluses on your feet
Remind you of how close you are to the earth
How much life your feet have trekked
Your thick soles the perfect canvas
For Gaia's gentle stroke of art

Let the blisters on your hand
Remind you of how hard you've worked
A silent show of your resilience
For every place where skin peels
Reveals layers of your story

Let the freckles on your skin
Remind you of how the Sun adorns you
Immersed in a blanket of light
Every spot a warm greeting
Inviting you to Nature's embrace

Let the stretch marks on your thighs
Remind you of how you've evolved
With subtle growth stored in flesh
Through all of life's changing tides
Your patterned waves have stretched to shore

Let the gray strands in your hair
Remind you of how blessed you are
To be kissed by lips of life
Every silver lock of love
A remembrance of your journey through time

Let the wrinkles under your eyes
Remind you of how much wisdom you hold
With folds of skin your pockets of life
Every crevice a knowing portal
Through which light seeps so freely

Let the blemishes on your body
Remind you of how alive you are
For all of your "imperfect" marks
Are life's signature that you have lived

We Flu Away

my body feels weak
my eyelids are heavy
i have aches and chills
breath no longer steady
my cheeks are flushed
my forehead lies hot
my nostrils are flaring
and dripping with snot
my arms are numb
my throat is dry
is this what it feels like
to slowly die?
my body feels weak
but my body is strong
these sensations
will not last long
because every sickness
i've ever faced
with some time
has gone away
the aches and chills
are my body's fight
the flushed cheeks
a reminder of life
thank you body
for keeping me safe
when *i* feel weak
you have my faith

Self Worth

to think I spent all this time
seeking validation
as though *beautiful*
only had meaning
when it came from your mouth

now I've discovered
I am beautiful
and I don't need a man
to make me believe it

Body Confidence

love your body in the morning when your stomach is
empty
in the middle of the day when you've just eaten a big
lunch
at the end of the night when you're full of food and
nourishment
love your body on days when you feel bloated
on days when you feel confident
on days when you feel the need to cover up
and days when you want to wear the cutest outfit

there is no such thing as a "bad day" for your body

it is completely natural that your body expands and
changes shape
over the course of a week
a day
and even a single meal

and that is incredible

honor your body in all its shapes and forms
don't compare yourself to others
and even more so
don't compare yourself to yourself
who you are in the picture with perfect angles and
lighting
is the same person as who you are in the mirror
when the sun is exposing every bit of your cellulite
and rolls

loving your body at every angle
in every light
every picture
and every day…
…is a learning process
but to love our bodies unconditionally
we must first release the pressure from ourselves
that our body always has to look like our best
moments on social media
*detach your current body from the social media version of your
body*
recognize that most of the posts you see of other
people
and of yourself
took many tries
many different poses
just the right place and time
so the light hits you in just the right way

remember
what you see online is a body captured in
one picture perfect moment
drop the expectation that your body needs to look
like that all the time
learn to love yourself even in those candid photos
when you weren't posing
or the sun wasn't hitting you in an ideal way

we are often our own biggest critics
yet the insecurities we struggle with
are features all people experience
though most people choose to not show

my dear, let them be seen

those features are beautiful
and real
and human
embrace them fully

once you start admiring who you are in all forms
you'll no longer feel the pressure
to meet a standard for yourself
that only you have created

imagine loving yourself from the eyes of someone
seeing you for the first time
the first thing you'd notice
is not that little dip in your hips that you're insecure
about
or the crease in your thighs
or the rolls on your belly
the first thing you'd notice is the way your eyes light
up
the way your smile glows
the way you do that sideways grin each time you say
something that makes you happy...

your body is simply the vessel through which your
spirit can experience the human world
nourish yourself with plenty of food without worrying
about how it will change your shape
your shape is bound to change
you will never look the same in one moment as you
will in the next...

and that only *adds* to your uniqueness and beauty

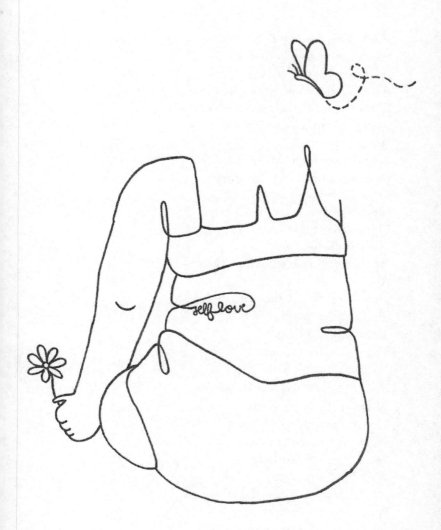

Search For Love

We search for Love
As though Love is hiding
And needs to be found
As though we can seek out Love
In the crevice of closed windows
And the bindings of open books
We say we want Love
So we look for it in people
Hoping to find it in the smile
Of another woman
Or the eyes
Of another man
We search for Love
As though Love is locked away
And the key is our desire
Held only by the passion
Of an open heart
That longs to find
This Love that hides

Do we search for our breath
When it flows so freely
Moving through our lungs
With ever-present ease?
Do we search for light
When the sun rises
And moves through the sky
With rays of promise?
Do we search for sound
When it fills our space
With loyal vibration
Wherever we go?

Like the air that fills our lungs with ease
The breath of Love exists all around
Inhale…
…Exhale
Let it all in
Why search for something that is already found?

~~~~~~~~~~~**Nature's Womb**~~~~~~~~~~~~

Her leaves, my limbs
Her whispers, my breath
Her colors, my spirit
Her heart, my chest

Thank you Mother Earth
From you we have birthed

~~~~~~~~~~~~~~~~~~~~~~~~~~~~~~~~~~~~~

Mother Nature's Plea

She is all around us

Everywhere we go, we experience Her beauty
We bathe in Her light
Play in Her tears
Swim in Her laughter

She is magnificent

It is Her voice that we close our eyes to when we put
our hands on our heart
It is Her light that we open our souls to as we look up
and feel Her presence

She is there

But we are taking Her for granted
While she keeps trusting us with Her spirit
We are handling it with no care
We are stealing away Her laughter
Instead of using it to harmonize with our own

So this is Her Plea
I am here for you, but I need you to be here for me
Because I am Earth, and I am your Home
But I do not feel at home in the Home that you've
created

The Lure of the Waves

I gravitate towards the ocean.
She lights me up. Sings to me. Empowers me to
channel my voice. Plays with me. Lets me drift and
flow with Her current. Her tender touch and mighty
caress. Her wild motion and gentle stillness. Her
passion that is felt through Her whispers of love as
the wind soars by.

I gravitate towards the ocean.
She pulls me in like the Earth pulls the moon. Wave
after wave, I am lured further into Her song. A voice
that is timeless, magnetic. A voice that is infinite,
filling all dimensions of space. Liquid meets eternal
soul. Physically. Spiritually.

I gravitate towards the ocean.

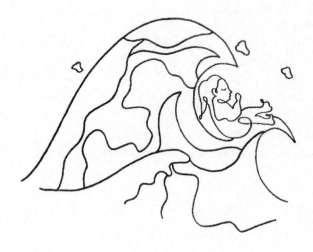

The Sound of Silence

What is the most beautiful sound you've ever heard?

Perhaps your mind wanders
To the distant sounds of Nature
The music of the morning birds
The flutter of their wings

Perhaps your mind wanders
To the bells of winter night
The laughter of the folks
The sizzles of the fire

Perhaps your mind wanders
To the pitter patter of the rain
The whispers of the snow kissing the Earth
The gentle swoosh of running water

All beautiful sounds indeed
Yet I must ask
Have you ever listened so intently...
At the bottom of a valley
The middle of a meadow
The depths of the woods

Have you ever listened so intently...
...that you heard the sound of Silence?

Silence
You hear nothing at all but everything at the same
time
Silence

The world opens a space for you to simply exist
Silence
Your own presence is the gravity that anchors you to
this abyss

The sound of Silence is the most beautiful sound I've
ever heard

For when we are surrounded by lights, chatter, and
noise
When we are surrounded by the distant rum of cars
The mellow hum of glowing lamps
The underlying buzz of society that is always on…
We forget what Silence sounds like

We forget that Silence exists

So when Silence finally fills your space
She embraces your entire being

Like a blanket that folds over time and holds it still
Like the world opening its doors to a deep unknown
Like God speaking to you through no sound at all

It is the pure bliss I feel in the rarity of this stillness
that has convinced me

When I hear the Sound of Silence…

I hear the Voice of God

Water's Wisdom

Have you ever looked out into the horizon
And saw no end?
Just water
Expanding into the farthest fields of your vision
Into the infinite space

The infinite space
It exists inside of you
Water heals us because it taps us into that space
That Flow of life that is boundless and so free

The wisdom of Water emerges from the persistence
of Her path
When boulders block streams
Water chooses another course to run
When Earth's edges are met
Water finds the courage to fall

At the end of it all
The obstacles that stand in Water's path
Are the very ones that carve out Her beauty

Like rivers that split into trickling creeks
Like ponds that drop into cascading waterfalls
There are no limits to Her infinite space

Learn from Her wisdom
There is nothing that can hold back your flow
When faced with boulders
Find a new path to explore
Know that the setbacks you face

Are the ones that create your waterfalls
From falling deepest, your beauty rises the most

So trust your own current to lead you
For when you flow like water
…boundless and free…
And expand yourself into that everlasting horizon…

You will find your infinite space

Rain

Heaven's embrace
Every drop a reminder
Of angel's wings
Wrapping us
In the golden warmth
Of her gentle kisses
Oh how my spirit
Becomes free
At the soft touch
Of divine love
A profound sense
Of recognition
That this bliss
Is what it means
To be alive
Bathe me
In holy waters
Let every tear
Be an invitation
To turn my face
Towards the sky
Lift my hands
In peaceful joy
And pray…

To be in rain
Is to be with God

The Sun and the Sea

oh how I love watching the sun set
oh how much peace it brings to me
to see the ball of fire melt to liquid gold
as it joins the horizon and kisses the sea
it's a love story unfolding before our eyes
souls searching for each other as time passes by
the ocean calls for the sun
and when she meets her lover…

the world explodes into marvelous color

Mama Kauai

Mama Kauai — you have shown us the most beautiful sunrises and the gloomiest skies. The most stunning waterfalls and the heaviest rains. The most serene seas and the wildest oceans.

What we see in Nature resembles the polarity we experience in Life. The rainbows of Mama Kauai cannot exist without Her storms. The sun within our souls cannot shine without our shadows.

Honor your highs and lows the way you celebrate Nature's clouds and clear skies. For Nature's spirit, and the spirit of Life, is not "perfect". Yet we love and cherish Her for everything She is.

Nature's Lullaby

Nature has Her own song
It's a lullaby that's as luring as the siren's call
Feels mystical and ever-present
While laying down and fully immersed
By the sounds of Earth's gentle murmur
The howls of the wind give the steady heartbeat
The crickets give the underlying pulse
The distant waves give the lingering harmonies
The brush of the leaves gives the soft rhythm
Every trace of life plays a tune
In Nature's sweet lullaby
May She sing me deep into my sleep
I'll listen as I close my eyes

~~~~~~~~~~**Wild Feminine**~~~~~~~~~~~~

we are women
with animalistic instincts
tamed by social norms
let's come back to our primal roots
and unleash our raw nature
crawl through the sand
use our hands and feet
roar under our breath
to let them know
that our wild feminine
is free from Her cage

~~~~~~~~~~~~~~~~~~~~~~~~~~~~~~~~~~~~~~

Sacred Love

we are learning how to love again. how to melt into the serenity of our deep acceptance for all that we are. how to make love with the life that cradles us into the safest embrace. how to spend time with our naked truth and worship every one of our insecurities that society deems unworthy.

society... they who profit off our belief that we are not enough. they who beg for us to compare ourselves to other women. they who call a naked body "sexy" before calling a naked body "sacred".

listen, we are learning how to love again. we are reclaiming our divine feminine and blessing each other with the love they hoped we'd never find. we are coming together as women with a new understanding of how pure our energy is. we are freeing our bodies, our spirits, our minds. we are not letting any judgment into our lives. we are seeking only the sweetest of loves, the kindest of hearts, the softest of souls...

and when you can look at us with a gentle smile on your face instead of a hunger in your eyes, we will know that you, too, are learning how to love again.

She Is Divine

Divine
She is divine

She who holds the energy of the cosmos in the flow
of her hips
And moves the weight of the world with the words
off her lips
She who grows her roots through the soils of the
earth
And within her spirit, plants the seeds of new birth
She who carries the nectar for the children of the land
And in the chaos of the night…
She takes her stand

For she is a woman
Existing in a time
When women are learning that they are divine
Breaking free from what does not align
No longer a part of the old paradigm

The old paradigm teaches us
That a woman cannot show her skin
Because being a "distraction" to men is a woman's
problem instead of a man's conditioning
The old paradigm says
That a woman must cross her legs
Because sitting comfortably with legs open is too
"suggestive"
The old paradigm tells us
That a woman has no freedom in the decisions she
makes over her body
Because a woman's body is a man's game…

Well let me tell you
The old and the new
They are not the same
We're becoming strong and we're ready to reclaim
The wild woman is no longer tame
She is using her voice
She is growing her mane
And the lioness has a fierce roar

For we are crushing down what existed before

Her skin embedded with crystals
Her body a treasure
It is not for your touch
It is not for your pleasure
She is wise like the sun that burns bright for ages
She adapts like the moon as it goes through its
phases
She howls like the wolves that run through the night
She ascends to the heavens as the angels take flight

Listen now
Do you hear her breath?
Do you hear her whispers crawling through your
chest?
Do you feel her rage?
Do you feel her thunder?
Do you feel your heart expanding with wonder?

She is alive
And she is in tune
Lays the ground for new life
Bleeds the fruit of the womb

She is the wild woman
And she is divine
May we now hold the space
For her light to shine

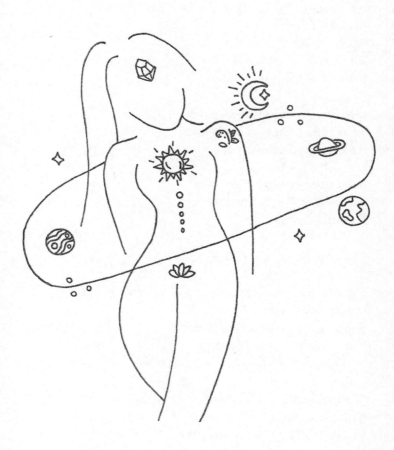

The Wonders of Her Waves

We call her Mother Earth
Divine feminine nature

Her mountains are a mystery
That only the sun meets
As it sets before dusk and kisses the valley
Bountiful hills
Rolling over the horizon
The shadows of womanhood
Contouring her creation

Her meadows are a gift
That only hummingbirds taste
As they feed on her nectar and transfer her pollen
Ponds of lotus
Reflecting colors of sunrise
The flowers of womanhood
Painting her gardens

Her oceans are a blessing
That only the clouds feel
As they drift over waters and gather her strength
Fierce tides
Sending white waters crashing
The power of womanhood
Washing her spirit

We may never understand
The wonders of her waves
But we call her Mother Earth
For her divine feminine nature

49

Primal Essence

Remember that we are all animals
Wild creatures roaming a tamed world...

Our primal instincts will not be caged
By society's structure and beliefs
Our mighty howls will not be drowned
By tall buildings and blinding streets

Our tender touch will not be shielded
By paved roads and concrete ground
Our roaring laughter will not be smothered
By bustling cars and busy sounds

No amount of human construction
Can destruct our true nature as human...

Human.

Who are we as humans?
Roaming this tamed world with wild hearts
Are we one with all living beings?
Or do subtle differences keep us far apart?

Our human superiority is self-imposed
By our two legs and an egoistic mind
When we strip away society's norms
We are all very much alike

So let's crawl back on our hands and feet
And remind ourselves of how it feels
To be free from made-up standards

By tuning in to what is real

We trace back to the same roots
And societal constructs can't divide
Our animal spirits which stay united
To the primal essence we feel inside

Remember that we are all animals
Wild creatures roaming a wild world...

Look Into My Eyes

Look into my eyes

In our eyes, we hold the portal to our inner worlds
Sometimes
We feel the urge to look away
Because that portal is a powerful one to open
It releases magnitudes of energy
That is captivating and frightening
At the same time

Look into my eyes

Let this energy allure you in
Rather than repel you away
Melt into the wild calm of our gaze
And if you feel hypnotized by the power
Of our two souls interlocking

Let yourself fall
Because maybe then
When you look into my eyes
You will find the pure stillness of spirit
Deep beneath the chaos of flesh

So if you feel called
To seek out the eye of the storm
And find refuge in the peace of my soul
While uniting with a piece of my soul
Then I'll tell you again...

Look into my eyes

Naked

In Her most sacred and primal state

Let us hold the space
For Her to find
Inside Her skin
The wild essence
Of *Human*

For Her to feel comfort
In the freedom
Of Her Naked Body
Without tagging it
To *Man*

For Her to be celebrated
In bareness
As pure expression
Of Her divine
Woman

Mother's Love

I think about myself as a mother sometimes

I think about how much joy it would bring
To feel another human being growing within
I imagine how much peace I would find
To touch the little hands and dimpled chin
I think about the connection I would feel
Knowing my soils nourish the seeds of life
And before even meeting this little human
I dream of the love that'd be blooming inside

And then...
I think about my own mother

I think about how she felt when I was her flower
And her love was the water that helped me grow
I envision how she watched her belly expand
As I stretched inside my very first home
I think of how she softly touched my face
And looked deep into my baby eyes
I imagine her leaving a kiss on my nose
While promising to love me through the end of time

When dreaming of my future children
A timeless love fills up my heart
May this serve as a reminder of my mother's love
Which she's felt for me from the very start

Nectar of Life

The nectar of life
Spills out from my womb
The space below my belly
Holds the home of a future
Which I have yet to meet
But already love

Let me tend to this home
Let me treat her with care
Let my thoughts be gentle
For our children rely
On our nurturing words
To fill the walls of their shelter
As they grow from within

My body is changing
As it always will
It expands and it shrinks
Leaving marks of strength
In the patterns of my skin

Instead of loathing these changes
Allow me to find
The blessings of womanhood
In every shape and form

For a mother's scar
Is a child's portal

And the space below my belly
Is a child's home

We Stand

Try to silence our voice
We will come back louder
Try to steal away our rights
We will stand strong as fierce warriors
Try to make us feel small
We will grow so big we can't be unseen
We are the foundation of life itself
You think you can cut through a woman
Who bleeds the very nectar from which you drink?

Free Spirits

go outside and dance in the rain
chase the sun
laugh with the waves
we are free spirits
experiencing life as our playground
give your inner child the freedom to play

There are times when the world around you simply stops and everything that is exists in the here and now. There are times when you feel called to let go of all your stresses or worries because you realize how insignificant they are to what truly matters. There are times when you take a step back from the hustle of work and school and fully experience the blissful nature of being present. There are times when you remember who you are, why you are here, why you have been given the blessing of waking up this morning...

To experience this beautiful life another day

Growing Up

As a child
I loved to dance in the rain
When it was pouring
I would run out and splash and giggle
Kick my feet in the puddles
Throw my hands in the air and laugh
Because the sky was an invitation
Asking me to come play

Now, when it rains
We have been trained to seek cover
Hide under rooftops
Wait patiently until it passes

As a child
I loved to roll in the sand
At the beach
I would build castles from the earth
Dig holes deep enough for me to fit
Twirl through the water
Then bury myself in golden dust

Now, at the beach
We lay on a towel
A piece of cloth guarding us from the earth
Because we cannot get too sandy
Or our cars won't stay clean

As a child
I loved to make friends with everyone
I would smile at students and play tag
Then chase other kids with jump ropes

Because "can you be my friend?" was all it took
To gallop through the schoolyard with someone new

Now, when we meet someone
We ask, "how are you?"
Without even turning our heads
And say, "good, thanks"
With our eyes still glued to the floor

Why is it that growing up
Means shrinking the energy that once filled us with so
much joy
Confining ourselves to formalities so we could
preserve our image
Controlling our primal instincts like laughter and
play?

Why is it that when we grow up
We are expected to lose the spirit that kept us a child?

What ages us is not time
Nor is it the number attached to our names
Rather, it is the mentality that our child-like spirit is
only present when we are children
When in reality
We are all children living in adult bodies

So go out and dance in the rain
Roll carelessly in the sand
Frolic with your friends
Cater to your inner child

Because if we forget the rules of adulthood

And listen to the cravings of our spirit
We will find that the child in us has always been
there
And then we will discover the most exciting truth...

There is no such thing as "Growing Up"

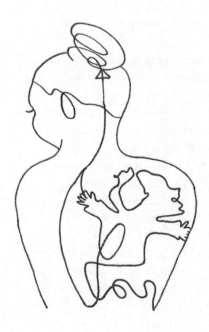

Romanticize Your Life

Romanticize your life
Slow down enough to find miracles in moments
Find laughter in silence
Find joy in despair
Imagine riding gondolas down the rivers of Venice
As you go on long walks around the town square
Be sure to inhale a breath when you find a flower
And lean down to take in the lovely scent
For everything in life is far more beautiful
When it is experienced with full intent

So when you're lying around with nothing to do
Imagine a choir inside of your room
With every voice singing a different tune
Perhaps these are the birds on your Sunday afternoon
And when a sweet butterfly passes you by
Imagine watching a fairy fly
Take time to absorb the sight
As her vibrant wings fill up the sky
When you're laughing hard with the person you love
Imagine Paris twinkling above
The dim streetlamps that glow for hours
Could take the place of the Eiffel Tower
And on the days you're by yourself at home
Imagine wandering the streets of Rome
Walk through your house with wondrous eyes
As though greeting the world for the first time

Now open your window and feel the air
While observing all the people pass
There's so much we forget to see
When we're moving through our life so fast

If we take the time to romanticize our lives
Then every moment could bring delight
With a little sprinkle of imagination
We can cherish all that's plainly in sight

Music

Listen to music
Let it fill your spirit so deeply
That your body becomes alive with a new life
One that melts into the sound
Melts into the rhythm
And surrenders to the flow

You are no longer attached to your next movement
Because the electricity of your own vessel moves you
The current of your own flow
Gives your body an energy that exists
Entirely on its own

Take a Breath

walk around barefoot
experience the earth between your toes
feel into your senses
let yourself get sandy
run and play
twirl through the water
bask in the sun

take a breath
live life in slow motion

all we need is in the here and now

Phoenix Rising

So be it
Let it consume me
Let it trickle into my bones
And set fire to every truth
That I've ever known
Let it flood through my blood
With boiling rage
Let it erupt
Ignite
Let my heart catch the flames

And then

Let my ashes
Sprinkle the earth
Lay blankets of embers
Every death a rebirth
An emerging phoenix
Golden slivers of hope
From broken pieces
New wings are restored
And from the depths of my soils
Allow flowers to rise
For what set me to fire

Also brought me to life

Gaia's Guidance

I've found it

That feeling deep in my heart that I've been searching
for all this time
That sense of sacred understanding that I am held by
the arms of the Mother
Who gave birth to all our spirits
And grew Her roots through the soles of our feet
That anchor us to this Earth...

God, I've found it

That pure knowing that we are all brothers and sisters
under the care of Gaia
Different branches extending from the same tree
Waters flowing from the eternal Source of all that can
be...

I feel Her breath on my lips as Her winds move
through my lungs
Inviting our voices to sing together as One
I've been searching so long to read the rhymes in the
clouds
So I've found poems in my heart and the music rings
loud
I am free

I am free
In the arms of the Mother
I've discovered my truth
To the Children of Gaia
This one is for you...

Let Her move through you and guide you towards
your gifts
For you are safe in this world to fully be seen
She holds space for you to explore who you are
There is no dream too big…
…There is no grass too green
Your flowers are rooted in Her nurturing soil
Dig into Her love as you plant the seed
Welcome Her spirit into your heart
And let yourself grow into who you can be
You are free

Sisters and brothers, children of the land
Trust in Gaia's guidance as your spirits expand
For Mother Earth never let go of my hand
As She led me towards finding *all that I am*

Be Present

take time every day
to *observe*
stop what you're doing
let out a deep breath
and just *observe*
notice your surroundings
pay attention to the sounds you hear
be fully present with the hums of the world playing its
rhythm
tune into your senses
what does it feel like
to sit in stillness
immersed in the moment
one with all that is?
what does it feel like
to take it all in
let go of the rush
and simply exist?

i choose a life of adventure, laughter, and play
i choose a life of excitement, spontaneity, and joy
i choose a life of unity, oneness, and peace

every day i choose the life of my dreams
and i will not settle for anything less

~~~~~~~~~~~~~Taste Your Tears~~~~~~~~~~~~~

sometimes
you need to taste your tears
to learn just how sweet
it feels to release
the emotions you've been storing inside

Gossip

why did i sit there
and listen
to every word she said
knowing very well
her words were like knives
that stabbed through the back
of the girl without eyes
what did she do
to deserve this from you?
what did she do
to deserve this from me?

i sat there
and listened

by listening
i was no better than her
my silence no better
than her evil words
just caused more pain
to what was already broken
another plunge through the wound
that lie freshly open

why didn't i speak up?
come to her defense?
why did i stay quiet
at her expense?
why didn't i say
that words could cause hurt?
why did i sit there

and listen to her?

we try to fit in
try to be something else
perhaps we listen to gossip
to protect ourselves
but that's not who i am
i'm better than that
no longer will let her
make you her doormat
i will not step on you
out of my fear
gossip only has power
when there are open ears...

and i am no longer listening

Sober Eyes

The world is moving in fast motion around me
Flashes of people yelling wildly
As they slur over the dizziness of their own choices
I feel like I'm not in my body
I've become an observer
Watching quietly as the room plays in full volume
I'm seeing a drunk world through sober eyes
Not a drop of liquor in my blood
But I still feel intoxicated

being high on life comes with no side effects

Wrinkles of Time

the wrinkles of time
tell stories of our rising
every crease in our skin
is a moment to unfold
with memories of life
embedded in gray hairs
and wisdom of ages
sunken deep below the eyes
time's tender touch
is raw in her beauty
but desperation
is quick to erase
that which is real
for that which is perfect
so the image of youth
is injected into minds
with needles that numb
the wrinkles of time

Complacency

we always want
what we don't have
and once we have it
we forget how much we wanted it

that happens with love
we get so comfortable
that the thought of forever
is no longer new
it's as fleeting of a thought
as a rushed "*i love you*"

remember when we were falling in love?
when we cherished every moment spent together
and our hearts fluttered from a prolonged gaze?
remember when we felt so blessed?
when we wanted so deeply to be the one
and we prayed that our love would last past a phase?

let's not take our love for granted
just because it's no longer new
let's not forget how much we wanted it
for we may lose it all if we do

is that what it will take?

Time Heals

It hurts
The pounding in my chest has yet to cease
It hurts
Allow me to heal from this heartbreak
Please

Why are my tears my new lullaby?
They've become more comforting than the kiss you
left on my lips
When you brought me to my door and mumbled
goodbye

Why are my cries the only sound that I hear?
They've become more consuming than the song you
left playing
When you uttered love's name as your deepest fear

Why are my whispers echoing through the night?
They've become more soft than the sweatshirt you
forgot to take with you
When you said it was time to move on with our lives

Time heals
Time heals
Time heals

Why are my tears starting to dry?
They're slowing down like your texts the last month
of our love
When it took you more than three days to reply

Why is my laughter ringing back in my life?
It's become more resounding than the voicemail you
left
When you told me you missed looking into my eyes

Why is the sun beginning to shine?
It's become more intense than the shake of my head
When you asked if our love could one day realign

Time heals
Time heals
Time heals

Now you want me back but it is too late
You say you're crying every day but I no longer relate

All I can do is wish you the best
And let you know that with time...

It will hurt less

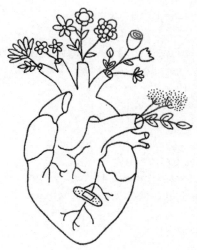

Saving Grace

You told me you loved me
In the same breath as you screamed out my flaws
You told me you cared for me
Moments after you sharpened your claws

You took the best in me
And shrunk it down
Forced me to dim my light
So yours could be found

Your fake apologies and promising words
Held me deeply in a trance
I lost more of myself every time
I gave you another chance

But despite it all, I am grateful
Because when I finally found the strength to run
I grew my beautiful angel wings
And flew straight to the sun

The stars opened their vast arms
And held space for me in the sky
They said it's okay to let it out
It is safe here for you to cry

I closed my eyes and put my faith
In the stars to help me heal
When my eyes opened, I saw *my* light
Shining through me like a golden seal

I then realized I am all I need
To be happy and to feel free
The darkness I passed through served as my guide
To the light that radiates within me

Thank you for breaking me
So I could put my pieces back in place
And learn just how capable I am
Of being my own saving grace

Once Upon a Time

Once upon a time
I met a man with a gentle heart
He treated me with much reverence
Or at least he did at the start

Listen as I share my story
Of how I slowly grew to see
The man who claimed enormous love
Actually had no love for me

On our first few dates together
We laughed all the nights away
When time came to say goodbye
My heart wished for you to stay

I was falling in love fast
And seemingly, so were you
On the day you told me that you loved me
I rushed to whisper, "love you too"

From then on, I went to sleep
Filled with thoughts of you and me
But perhaps I created a version of you
That only existed in my dreams

As time went on, our flame went out
And truth be told, our romance died
With it, so did the man I loved
As you revealed a different side

That's when all the hurt began
Sweet words turned to ruthless cries

The smallest things would set you off
As you transformed before my eyes

But even as you called me names
And never let me feel heard
You still said you loved me so
And professed that I was your world

When I finally gained the courage
To tell you that I wished to leave
You looked at me with shocked eyes
As though you were in disbelief

You told me I would never find
Someone who loves me quite like you
As if you chose to close the blinds
On all the yelling and abuse

After enduring such a loveless love
I thought I had no happy end
My dreams now were filled with thoughts
That Prince Charming was pretend

But then he came along...

He got to know me for my truth
And listened to every word I said
He whispered notes of affirmation
For every tear that I shed

He loved me with such a passion
He cradled my heart in his hands
And even when we misaligned
He always worked to understand

Our communication was so conscious
And every week, we would reflect
We held the space to share our hearts
While listening with deep respect

His love was always soft and kind
He never once raised his voice
And even with much on his plate
He made me feel like his top choice

He held the car door every day
And buckled me in with a kiss
He treated me like a queen
I've never felt a love like this

He assured me that I was so safe
He'd protect my heart through all of time
He empowered me to share my voice
And worshiped me like I'm divine

After years of this nurturing love
I trust it's more than just a phase
It's the purest love I've ever known
Heaven lies in his embrace

All the darkness turned to light
Truly all the stars aligned
Now I have forever with
The love you said I'd never find

Holding On and Letting Go

I'm trying to move on
This is all for the best
I told myself this would be the last time
But letting you go
Feels like clearing my thoughts
With hundreds of memories still on my mind

I know in my head
We're not meant to be
I've convinced myself we're not the right fit
But trying to move on
Is a difficult task
When my heart has yet to fully commit

Why is it that
The word "baby"
Still slips from my mouth as though it's your first
name
Is it wrong of me
That I still want to call
Even though we agreed that things need to change?

There will be days
When I'm getting by fine
And I don't feel too hurt by us being apart
But then I'll remember
The cute way you grin
And you'll find your way back to my mind and my
heart

So even though
I'm trying to move on

My love for you will always be known
At the end of it all
I can't help but feel
Like coming back to you is coming back home

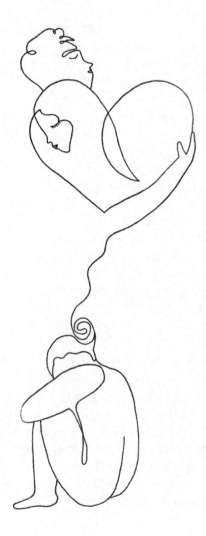

The Power of Nothing

You thought she was quiet
Because she kept her voice in
But silence is sometimes the loudest sound
And her silence was the spell that caused you to
break
It caused your power to be swept away
As your whole body was aching for a response
To the words you sent like flashes of fire down her
spine
But you were met with...

Nothing

And so you called her quiet
That was the only word you could muster among the
loudness of her silence
That pierced your bones as you tried to grasp onto
the power that was no longer yours
She reclaimed it as hers
The moment she responded with...

Nothing

See, while you were hoping she would yell to her
defense
And add more fuel to the fire you were spitting out
You didn't know it was burning your tongue to keep
talking to a woman who no longer heard you
For she had realized her worth and in return to your
anger she met you with peace
That was far more a stab through your ego
Than any fight would have been

Because you wanted a fight
But what you got was…

Nothing

So you said she was quiet
You said she kept her voice in
But really, you heard her voice louder than ever
Her silence had stripped you away from the only
power you knew
And as the quiet shrunk you down, she finally grew
Into the delicate rose with thorns up its stem
A fierce warrior hiding behind gentle brown eyes
I hope you'll never again find it a surprise
When a woman brings up her shield instead of taking
out her sword
And cuts through with silence instead of fighting with
words
The power you held is no longer yours
Because she became everything
When she gave you…

Nothing

Anchor

Your love is my anchor
It makes me feel secure
It holds me strong
Through the lashing winds
And stabilizes me
Through life's changing currents

Your love is my anchor
It makes me feel trapped
It pulls me down
To the ocean's depths
And prevents me from drifting
Towards my own path

Your love is my anchor
My steady embrace
It brings me comfort to know
I'm attached and I'm safe

Your love is my anchor
It locks me in place
I'm fighting to swim
But I'm stuck in your brace

Is it time to release?
Is it time to escape?
Is it time to believe
In my own strength?
Is it time to find clarity?
Is it time to find truth?
Is it time to find peace

In who I am without you?

Your love is my anchor
It is sheltered and safe, but it is also unfree…

How do I let go of your anchor
When it's made me afraid of what lies in the sea?

Blank Pages

I've read all the pages of your story
But when I turned to the next chapter
We left it blank
Escaped memories that wanted to be lived
Yet only their illusions have come to life
Because now you're a stranger
An empty book
Even though I've read your pages a hundred times

Is this it?
Is this how it ends?

I've gotten used to waking up by your side
I remember the scent of your breath when you
wished me good morning
And the taste of your mint when you kissed me good
night

How do I go from knowing everything about you…

Like the way your eyes glimmer when you are in love
And the way your lips quiver when you are in pain
The way you like to spend time in your home to
recharge
But you'll throw your shoes off to go dance in the
rain

How do I go from knowing everything about you…

Like the wrinkles on your face that show up when
you smile

And the dreams in your heart that you want to fulfill
To suddenly pretending like everything we shared
Has frozen in time and since become still

Our moments together have turned into tales
But those moments are still very real and alive
The broken clock that has become still
Will start ticking again as our memories revive

Now I close my eyes and you're no longer there
Erased from my life but not erased from my mind
For when a book you've read clears out from your
shelf...

The stories you've learned are still left behind

Broken

don't sit there and tell me
to pick up my pieces
as though my heart
is made of glass
you threaten to leave
what do you expect?
for me to chase you?
beg you to stay?
kneel at your feet
so you can feel wanted?
i see right through
your twisted games
i'm not here to play the part
so instead of telling me
to pick up my pieces
mend your own fragile heart …

I'm not broken

we went from a breakup
to a breakdown
to a *breakthrough*

The Beggar on the Street

I've become friends with the beggar on the street

When people pass by
They shoot him a glance
And speed up their pace
As he holds out his hands

They don't give him money
They claim he'll "use it for drugs"
Meanwhile he sleeps on cold pavement
With critters and bugs

I cannot lie
I was one of the many
I hid my wallet in my pocket
When he asked me for pennies

I walked away thinking
This man just pretends
But then I heard his voice behind me
"All I want is a friend

"I have been here for months
"The world has left me estranged
"Spending every day alone
"Will make any man deranged

"I'm not a thief nor a victim
"Won't take your clothes nor your car
"I'm just as human as you
"Beneath the dirt and the scars"

So I sat down with him
Listened to what he had to say
He shared his life story
Then together we prayed

He once had a family
A decent job and a house
But he lost his life to heartbreak
When illness fell upon his spouse

Between tears he recalled
How her life withered away
As more medical bills
Piled up every day

I can't help but feel
Heavy guilt settle in
As I remember the fear
I projected onto him

Although he's labeled a beggar
We have all become blind
To the realness in spirit
That he carries inside

The man who gets so much hate
Is here because of his love
He gave everything for his wife
Who joins our prayers from above

I've become friends with the man on the street
He is much more a friend than a beggar to me

Your Chance

what would you do if you woke up tomorrow
and you were the only person left on earth?
every person you ever loved
every person you ever cared about
every person you ever wished to connect with…
…*gone*

what would you do if you could rewind the time
and come back for a day
just one day
to say the things you wanted to say
to get in one more "*i love you*"
to approach the person you've always hoped to talk
to?

would it take losing everyone to realize this is your
chance?

the truth is
this isn't just a thought
you never know how much time we've got
so treat every day like it's the last
in real life…
you can't rewind to the past

Death's Dying Wish

What if Death's dying wish
Was to experience life once more?
What if Death consumes our spirits
In the hopes of reviving His own?
Can we really be angry at Death
When He too longs to come alive?

Life and Death

i imagine death sometimes
i imagine what it's like to close your eyes
and never see the world again
is it like falling asleep
or do you see flashes of light as you go?
death is the one story that could never be told
for those who know it
lose the mouthpiece
through which we absorb it
it frightens me to think
how everything goes on without you
the world wakes up to a day
like any other
except you're no longer aware
of what that day will look like
how that day will unfold
what that day will be
or are you?
we all have our own beliefs about death
we've created stories
from the stories of the untold
opened heaven's gates
to find comfort for the old
some say our spirits will still be alive
but nobody knows
what it's really like to die
our thoughts shape our reality
as all things in life
we make the experience
from which we survive

maybe death, too, is ours to create

maybe life and death are one and of the same

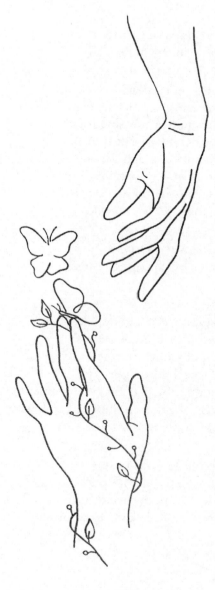

Changing Times

As humans
We gravitate towards our tribe
We find comfort in the mere notion of *us*

We build homes on the backs of people
Who work together to mold the clay
We form communities and sing together
As we bring our children out to play
We discover family through the sound of laughter
And the comfort of our neighbor's smile
Life involves a sense of *us*
When we live together in the wild

Loneliness is a novel condition
Plagued upon us by changing times...

We now spend more work and energy
Seeking validation from a handheld device
Than we spend time holding hands
With the very people who brought us to life
Where did all the children go?
They're trapped inside playing video games
More obsessed with their number of followers
Than meeting people face to face

There was a period in our past
When we did everything with one another
Let's not allow our modern screens
To steer us away from finding each other

The old saying goes
It takes a village to raise a child

So now I can't help but ask…
What does it take to rebuild a village?

Friends

we're holding on by delicate strings
friends only because that's all we know
maybe it's time for us to accept
it's best to let each other go

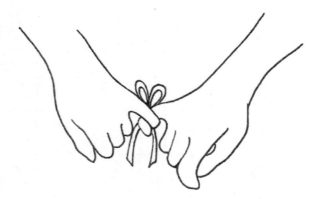

Betrayal

betrayal feels like walking out into fields of grass
and being met instead with shards of glass
forgiveness is the trust to take another step
with feet that are already cut and swollen

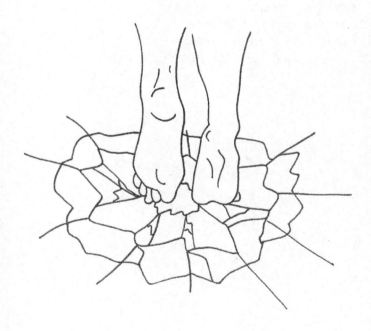

Dear Stress

dear stress,
i've met you many times before
yet every time i see you
you come to me in different form
why is it that i know your name
yet you still feel as if brand new?
i've learned all of your qualities
yet i still feel so drained by you
there's a reason we so often meet
i won't accept your greeting as defeat
maybe i'm just meant to see
that you don't have control of me

i'm depressed
she said
the wise woman paused
is that what you tell yourself?
yes
another pause
then of course that's what you are

Your Life Matters

I'm hiding
I'm curling myself up into a little ball and shrinking so
small that I can't even be seen by my shadow on the
ground
I'm hiding because I don't know who I am right now
and I need to disappear so I can be found
I'm running
I'm running because I'm trying to rediscover the
person I was and I'm hoping I'll find her somewhere
on my path
The faster I run, the sooner I'll heal that piece of my
heart that is aching for the love I once trusted would
last
Faster
Faster
I'm losing my breath
Faster
Faster
I won't let myself rest
I'm hearing high-pitched sounds and seeing fading
lights
Darkness seeping in through the cracks of my mind
I'm running, but my legs are slowly giving out
The voices in my head are getting too loud…

Suddenly, it stops
Everything stops

Hello?
Can anyone hear me?

I cry out into an empty space

Where am I?

This feels like a lonely and mysterious place

I imagine a lot of us feel this way at times
When we're deep in the dark space of our wandering
minds
Lost in the depths of the endless abyss
Questioning the purpose of all that is

Now I'm alone and I'm faced with a choice
To come out of the dark or stay lost in the void
Will it be worth it to even try?
Why should I stop hiding? Why?

It's just you and me, God
I'm listening...

The answer is really quite simple, my dear
Your life matters
There's a reason you're here

Imagine the way the flowers grow towards your
outstretched hand
And the winds part as you're walking by
Imagine the way your father smiles at the sound of
your laugh
And your mother weeps at the sound of your cry
Imagine the way the Universe moved
To make space for your spirit to be set free
Imagine the way the moon and the sun
Welcomed you in when you came to be

*You see, the moon and the sun are like the dark and
the light
You need both to form the wonders of this magical
night
A rising sun appears after all the fallen stars
Move through your shadows to find the glow of your
heart*

My pace has slowed as I feel more peace
The whispers of God have put my mind at ease
The words keep echoing in my head
"Your Life Matters," the Universe said

That's when I finally begin to realize
I don't need to run from my shadows to discover my
light
With a deep breath, I open my eyes…

I'm ready to live this beautiful life

Divine Union

Our two souls entangled
Our two minds aligned
Our two hearts beating
Our spirits intertwined

In sacred embrace
We sing to the sun
Hums of the two
Uniting as one

thank you for loving me
it is the greatest gift I've ever felt
to be loved by you

God's Art

I've met a Man who speaks of the Woman
As if she is an angel herself
Created by the hands of heavens
Descending by the rays of light
He speaks of her body not as a source of pleasure
But as the elixir of life
That is just as one with nature
As the crystalline waters from which she rises

I've met a Man who speaks of the Woman
As if she is a portal to the divine
Pure as the crisp air that fills our lungs
Carved from the white marble of ancient times
He speaks of her energy as though it heals humanity
Her touch as soft as a feather landing in stillness
Her gaze as sacred as the sun's colors
Before inviting the night sky

I've met a Man who speaks of the Woman
With a love as serene as melting ice
She feels safe in his holy presence
He holds the space for her to be free
His tender masculine protects her spirit
And Love comes with gentle eyes
As he closes his and still whispers,
"God's art"

First Love

I love you.

I love you I love you I love you.

I could say it a thousand times more and I still won't
get over the way it tingles the roof of my mouth as
the words come out.

Is it silly that I cover my eyes and giggle each time I
say it out loud?
Is it silly that my skin crawls and tummy flutters when
I sense you feel it too?
Is it silly that I feel like I'm emerging into the world
again when I'm with you?

Loving you feels like warm apple cider on a snowy
day
Loving you feels like an awkward laugh when I have
no words to say
Loving you feels like sinking into the deepest
embrace
Loving you feels like melting away into time and
space
Loving you feels like a dream I fall asleep to every
night

Loving you feels right. Loving you feels right.

So maybe one day, when I say "I love you"
I won't giggle from the novelty of it being true
Maybe one day, when I say "I love you"

You'll look at me and say, "I love you too"

Three Words

When I say *I love you*
What I'm really saying is
You make my inner child feel safe
Time slows down when I'm by your side
In your caramel eyes, I see my future
Holding hands while dressed in white
Your love is my sweet sanctuary
I melt into the love that you provide
I want to wake up with you every morning
And fall asleep with you every night
When the sun hides behind the gray
Your smile brings me all the light
A warmth lingers from your touch
A spark that's ready to ignite
You bring me such a sense of ease
You inspire all the songs I write
I feel like you're my family
You're such a big part of my life
I could say a million things
Of how this all feels so right
Just know that when I say *I love you*
There's so much those three words imply

Seeing Red

I've never seen the color red like this
It's vibrant and beautiful
Luscious and bright
I've gifted my heart
Love has gifted me eyes
A whole new lens through which I perceive
The oak tree that dangles
Is a new shade of green
The flowers I've passed by so many times
Radiate now with a soft yellow light
The clouds that once were a dull tone of gray
Glisten with blue as they leak the sun rays
Everything looks like it's changed from before
So much of the world I now want to explore
Colors I never knew could exist
It's your Love that's making me see all of this

In Love

yes
i'm in love
is it easy to tell?
do you see what I feel
when my heart starts to swell?
do you hear the way
my breath picks up its pace?
do you see the glow
that I get in my face?
you said
you're in love
without any delay
tell me
what is it
that gave me away?

Muse

Before I met you
I would pick up a pencil and begin to write
But I'd be stuck for days trying to get one line
Of prose onto my empty sheet
Writer's block
Is what they called it
I referred to it as my defeat
I felt at times like giving up
With no inspiration to move along
But when I met you
Everything changed
As you found your way into every song
You became my pencil
You became my journal
You became the ink that splattered my pages
You were my story
You were my book
You flew me through all the writing stages
With so much emotion I hoped to convey
Not writing for months turned to writing every day
What lived for long as an empty sheet
Regained its life as you set me free
Love is the cure for a vacant mind
You embraced every crevice and filled every line
Your love was my muse that caused me to find
The words that would've been left behind

Love's Deceit

I imagined an idea of what Love should be
Based on the books I have read
And the stories that unfolded on my screen
The images of Love still play in my head

Slow dancing as the sun sets over a distant hill
Laughing until the sun rises again
Holding hands down a snowy lane as time stands still
Flipping through memories from way back when

I smiled as the story ended with a kiss
Meaning they found the one in each other
Wondering when I could experience this
I flipped through more novels so I could read another

With every *I love you* that felt so real
It became easier to neglect
All the rehearsing it took to create
This Love that seemed so perfect

This portrayal of Love led me to believe
That the sunsets and laughter were a constant
guarantee
Now I've learned I was simply naive
Love is rarely what the stories make it out to be

Rather, Love is a balance between two entangled
souls
Each with their own beliefs and thoughts
Carrying unique visions and goals
Will they end up connected or stuck in a knot?

Just like a game of tug-of-war
Both must hold on to reach a stable place
When hands start slipping and grasping for more
You must trust in each other's lasting embrace

If one starts pulling too much of the rope
The balance is shattered and problems arise
Slowly, you start losing hope
As there is no win if it's one partner's prize

Between the tender moments and loving gaze
There are arguments and there are tears
Between the compliments and giddy praise
There are frustrations and there are fears

It's okay if your Love isn't a movie scene
Most of those stories are incomplete
It's better to write your own story than to be
Caught in the web of Love's Deceit

So go into Love without expectations
Of what it must live up to
Start with a blank page and no hesitation
Let your souls paint both yellows and blues

For when I went into Love with my mind set
On what I believed it should be
I fell more in love with this idea of Love
Than I fell in love with you and me

Your Person

in just two months
i felt
what i hadn't felt
in our two years
it's not a matter of time
when you find your person
you will know

I Still Love You

I crave the way your gentle hand feels on my skin
So I sense your touch in the breeze
And find your lips in the wind

I yearn to be held again in your sweet embrace
So I feel your warmth in the sun
And find your arms in the rays

I long for your ocean eyes to meet mine once more
So I find your gaze in the sea
As light reflects off the shore

I hope to hear your love once again in your words
So I find your voice in the sky
Through the songs of the birds

You see, darling, you'll always be in my life
In the wind and the sun
And the sea and the sky

Twin Flames

it is beautiful seeing you in love
it's nothing like I've ever seen before
when you're together
the world melts away
as if looking into each other's eyes
opens a portal into the heavens
you find heaven within each other
it is divine
you've created a kingdom from your love
a palace of pleasure
every moment a ceremony
every day a celebration
your children will be angels
pillars of light
for only light can be born
from a love so divine
past the doors of your temple
your hearts are held safe
in the comforting nest
of eternal embrace
you let yourselves fall
into sweet gentle kisses
with the world looking in
at your love from a distance
it is free like the dove
that sings through the sky
you're united in joy
and together you rise
two spirits intertwined
you are one and of the same
let the passion ignite
for you've found your twin flame

The Love You Showed Me

I'm grateful you loved me
Because from your love I learned what love can be
I learned just how pure and kind a love can feel
You showed me a love that fills every crevice
Seeps in like light shining through stained glass
You showed me a love that is tender and soft
A pillow of feathers to lay my head
When saltwater tears spill into rivers
You showed me a love that is full of life
Dancing freely through open air
Inviting the wind to let go of its breath
I found the love of God within your spirit
And from that, I've found the love of God
So even though our love didn't last...

The love you showed me always will

The Ocean Remembers

The ocean carries my memories
In the footprints of the sand
I leave a piece of my story
My first kiss now a whisper in the wind
My bare body now a breath of the earth
The ocean remembers
The first time
I looked in your eyes
And knew I found love
The ocean remembers
Parting the skies
To show us the light
That beams from above
Remember that night
We held hands
In the glow of the moon
And we became one?
Remember that night
We prayed to the clouds
And heavens opened
To welcome the sun?
The ocean remembers
Every memory
Every thought
Every time I hummed your name
The ocean remembers
Every tear
Every laugh
Every lyric that I sang
It's all here
I feel it now
I'm walking with the wisps of wind

Grains of sand
Deep inhale
Soft and tender life within
I love you too
She heard my voice
Surrendered me to her flow
Bathed in waters
Soaked in love
Nostalgic ripples far below
She holds my memories
Timeless time
She keeps them safe
For long as can be
The wisp of the wind
A remembrance of love
Is but a return
To you and me

My Love

My love

How sweet it feels to call you so
Breathing tunes into your ear
Citrus walls from candle glow
Ocean scents where you appear
My soft love plays loud strings
Raise orchestras at the sound of

My love

Has me dancing in new places
French songs parade off walls
Of empty rooms and glass vases
Laughing as the night falls
Spinning slow with limbs of honey
Melting deep into the arms of

My love

Hugging tightly from behind
Aprons filled with flour patches
Like roots our bodies intertwined
Striking flames with feeble matches
Among the grandest symphonies
All I can hear is still

My love

i can't wait for the day i melt into your arms
and know i can stay there forever

28 (two infinity)

it doesn't matter
if i've loved you for ten days
or loved you for ten years
i will always look at you
and remember
how blessed i am
to have you in my life

Where Skin Meets

Leave trails of honey
Down the back of my spine
Sweet droplets of nectar
Taste beads of divine

A palette of olive
And red stroke of lips
Chills running like water
Soaked deep in the bliss

Soft tickles of whispers
And sharp waves of heat
Fast flashes of fire
At the place where skin meets

Offer scents of fresh lilac
In the trace down my wings
Electric shocks of desire
From the warmth this love brings

All five senses heightened
Bodies flowing in sync
Sudden rupture of flames
Flying close to the brink

Now pulsing with wonder
Spirit wild with feeling
Nothing quite like the touch
Of another human being

It Was Worth It

maybe we were meant to experience the love
so we could trust what awaits after the pain
maybe we had to reach the highest peak
to understand what exists beyond the deepest valley
for when we admire stars from a distance
we see a few specks of light in the sky
it is far more profound when we know
that among those specks lies the Universe

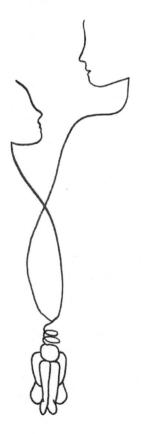

every shooting star I've ever wished on has led to you

The Seasons of Love

There was once a boy I thought I loved

He was my late nights in a car driving nowhere type
of love
My picnics at the beach during sunset type of love
My twirling in the rain with our clothes on type of
love
My getting lost with each other in the moment type of
love

There was once a boy I thought I loved

He was my dancing through the night with no worries
type of love
My losing track of time type of love
My running to Denny's at midnight type of love
My laughing until my lungs hurt type of love

There was once a boy I thought I loved…

But now I wonder, was it really love?

Was it really love if it came with no pain?
Was it really love if we never learned to mend
sorrow?
Was it really love if we never healed each other's hurt?
Was it really love if we never held hands through
hardship?

Love isn't always a 2am drive to the ocean and a 6am
nap at the beach

Love isn't always a candlelit dinner and a moonlit
stroll
Love isn't always a slow dance at sunset and a kiss in
the rain

So I wonder... was it really love?

The love felt by a long-married pair is different from
the love felt by newlyweds
The love felt by a high school couple is different from
the love felt by college grads
The love felt by me now is different from the love felt
by me then
The love felt by me tomorrow will be different from
the love felt by me today

Love is changing
Love is evolving
Love is growing
Love is trying

It does not matter whether you can justify the love
you once felt with the version of love you feel now

Love is
Love simply is

There was once a boy I know I loved

Long Distance

my love,
I see you in every constellation
yet you are constellations away
I feel your hand as though it's interlocked with mine
yet when I reach for you
I'm grasping onto air
I feel your breath as though your face is before me
yet I only see you
when my eyes are closed
your kisses fly with the wind
of every long windowless drive
and your voice plays in my heart
like the lyrics of a song that are never forgotten
you are everywhere at once and nowhere at all

my love,
I wish extending my hand meant reaching for yours
I wish feeling your breath meant you're whispers away
I wish waking up meant you're by my side
but until that is
your kisses I feel in the wind
and the lyrics of your voice that ring from afar
are enough to get me towards the day
that our love will exist beyond the stars

I Miss You

i crave moments of stillness
to see you more clear
the most silent mind
is where you appear
oh how i wish
that you could be here
with me in my heart
i miss you
my dear

whenever you miss me, look at the moon
send words through your gaze
and speak through the ethers

we are two entangled souls
we'll find our way back to each other
in every lifetime

Puzzle Piece

my head sits on your shoulder
as though the space was carved just for me
my hand curls into yours
as though our hands were designed to meet
my back curves into your lap
as though it was made to be my seat
my heart rests against yours
as though our two souls share one beat
i can't help but notice, my love
you fit just like a puzzle piece
maybe that's a sign for us
that our love is truly meant to be

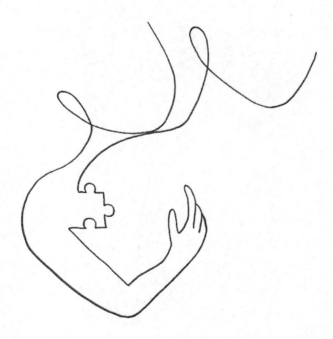

Together

when I met you
everything became easy
the world became weightless
as if I could finally let go of my breath
and move slow with the rhythm of life
every fear I had dissipated
into thin air
for just knowing I had you
to always be there
was enough to get me through anything
the future doesn't scare me anymore
we're building this life
together now

i have a lifelong of loving you
what's the rush?

Prayer for Love

I pray for a love that is real
I pray for a love that stands strong through the tests
of time
I pray for a love that is soothing
Like a warm cup of chamomile when the clock rings
nine
I pray for a love that is honest
I pray for a love that stems from utmost loyalty and
truth
I pray for a love that is eternal
Like a magical sip from the fountain of youth
I pray for a love that is gentle
I pray for a love that shows empathy and deep
concern
I pray for a love that is giving
Like an act of service that expects no return
I pray for a love that is nurturing
I pray for a love that makes me feel protected and
safe
I pray for a love that is affectionate
Like a long hug that melts into sweet embrace

God tells us to be patient with love
So I will happily wait for years
As long as when the time does come...

I find the answer to all my prayers

I know you love me...
...*but are you still in love?*

My Future in Your Eyes

In your eyes, I find my future
I see my life flash before me in the twinkle of your
gaze
As the sky turns to red, I see us wrapped in embrace
I see the cute nights of giggles and deep nights of
tears
I see us shedding our layers and revealing our fears
I see us building our careers and working hard
towards degrees
While spending slow mornings sipping our tea
I see us growing together as spirits aligned
I see us choosing each other for the rest of our lives
I see you smiling as you slowly get down on one knee
And promise that you will forever love me
As I leap towards your arms, I see me crying with joy
I see you sharing your love with your deep, soothing
voice
I see us traveling together and discovering new places
I see our bodies intertwined in all sorts of spaces
I see us moving into our very first home
I see us decorating our porch with small yellow
gnomes
And when the time comes, I see us buying a crib
To welcome our firstborn into our bliss
I see you holding my hand while you give me a kiss
In awe that our love created life's greatest gift
I see you bringing your inner child out to play
As you shower the babies with love every day
I see us sending our kids to their first day of class
Holding back tears because they grow up so fast
I see us eventually returning to an empty nest
With only the company of each other left

I see us leaning on each other when times get tough
Trusting that the love we've built will always be
enough
And one day, when we're both frail and gray
I see us still dancing the nights away
For a love like ours transcends all time
No matter how old, we'll always love what's inside

My dear, I truly see my whole life
Every time I look into your eyes

~~~~~~~~~~~~~~~**Light Leaders**~~~~~~~~~~~~~~~

let's dance together under the stars
and allow the constellations to be our guide
to the powerful energy of the cosmos
and the galactic potential we feel inside

~~~~~~

Angels on Earth

we are angels on earth
beams of laughter and love
leaving traces of light wherever we go
we are flowers rising
from eternal Source
in heaven's embrace as our petals grow
we are peacemakers
and energy shifters
spreading joy through all the land
we are the happy ones
returning to bliss
allowing love's frequency to expand
we bring forth the new paradigm
we activate new truth
in every being, we bring out the divine
we open the portal
to infinite love
inspiring heaven's light to shine
this is it
we've found our place
the path is clear as can be
for when we walk
the path of love
Love follows *us* eternally

Lessons of the Universe

We are always being guided
Everything that happens to us is happening for us
Every challenge is here to serve us
The energies we give are the energies we receive
Our gratitude becomes our lived experience
The Universe listens to the thoughts we put out
So don't ever spend a moment in doubt
That we are always being guided

Be Light

we *see* light

we see it in the rays of the sun that glow off our skin
we see it rise behind the sea as the morning begins
we see it shimmer off puddles as early birds take
flight
we see it flashing through fires that burn through the
night

what does it mean to *be* light?

can you be the rays of sun that lighten somebody's
day?
or the colors of sunrise that make the world less
gray?
can you be the bright sparkle someone sees in the
mirror?
or the glow that makes the darkest night crystal clear?

my dear, we all have a light inside
what you do with that light is yours to decide
just know, all the light in this world that you see
is simply a reflection of who you can be

Affirmations

I am abundant
I am innovative
I am strong
I am kind
I am loved
I am Love
I am influential
I am beautiful
I am eternal
I am intelligent
I am adventurous
I am generous
I am conscious
I am charismatic
I am connected
I am expressive
I am overflowing with joy
I am grateful to be alive
I am capable of getting through challenges
I am exactly where I need to be
I trust the Universe that everything happens for a reason
I listen to my intuition
I spread love to everyone around me
I make an impact *just by being me*

Among the Stars

Imagine…

We are the eyes through which the Universe looks inwards upon itself. The portals through which the Universe experiences its own existence. The conscious connection between the Universe and all that is.

We may be just a speck in the galaxy
But we are one among the stars
And with every conscious being
That enters the cosmos…

The Universe awakens even more

Integration

I don't need to leave the earth every time I meet the
clouds
I can stay grounded in who I am
While exploring the infinite space of all that is
My spirit self and human self do not exist as a duality
They both share the commonality of co-creating my
reality

Shower Thoughts

do you ever think about the people who will become
significant parts of your life but you haven't met yet?
do you ever wonder what they're doing right at this
moment?

it's profound to imagine that most of the people in
your future life are coexisting with you right now
we are sharing the same field of space and time...
we are all creating ourselves in this collective
consciousness together

sometimes
when I cross paths with a new person
instead of seeing them as a stranger
I recognize them as someone who's existed on this
earth with me through all the same moments
and I wonder what their life story is

it's beautiful that we all have so much that makes us
who we are
and every single one of the 7 billion+ of us is here
simultaneously under the same sun

wow

We Are One

Sisters and Brothers
We're all experiencing
This beautiful Earth at the same time
Don't you see how magical it is
That all our lifelines have aligned?

Of all the many thousand years
Our human selves could come to be
We've found each other in this moment
A sliver of eternity

All the people you've cared about
And all the people you're yet to love
Are here on this Earth with you
Or joining from the skies above

It really is miraculous
To think of every human here
Together under the same stars
United by our joys and tears

We weren't meant to start wars
Let's drop our swords and end the fight
We're all children of the moon
Bringing peace throughout the night

Sisters and Brothers
Let's join our hands
And lift our voices towards the Sun
Let's freely sing the words of love
We are One. *We are One.*

~~~~~~~~~~~~~~~**To Be Happy**~~~~~~~~~~~~~~~

I pray for the day
Every person can experience
The simple bliss of being human

~~~~~~~~~~~~~~~~~~~~~~~~~~~~~~~~~~

just a reminder that you are a sacred expression of
love and light and you have a beautiful purpose in this
world that you are fulfilling simply by being present
and being you

I Love Life

I love the way the waves make my hips flow
I love the way the setting sun makes my skin glow
I love the way the trees call for me to dance
I love the way the blooming fields let my heart
expand
I love the way the clouds make my soul feel at peace
I love the way the rising tide rushes up my knees
I love the way the hills bring my spirit out to play
I love the way the crystal lakes shimmer as I pray

I love the way I find beauty in everything I see
I love the way loving life is what sets me free

What's Now

We're always in motion
There is a turbulence in our ways
Lost in the wind
We're pushed forward to what's next

What's Next?
We woke up with the sun and took a morning stroll
but
What's Next?
We achieved a short-term goal in our personal
journey but
What's Next?
We went out with a friend we're just starting to know
but
What's Next?

Why are we so attached to what's next instead of
focusing on what's now?

See the wind that is pushing us forward
May indeed be just a breeze
Whether we are leashed to the motion of the wind
Or surrendered to the stillness of the breeze
Is up to the strings that we ourselves have tied
For this seeming motion of life
Is an illusion of our own turbulent mind

So instead of being swept away by your wind
Close your eyes and simply imagine...

What's Now?

We woke up with the sun and feel the morning rays
warm our skin
What's Now?
We are overcome with gratitude for the milestone we
reached in our personal journey
What's Now?
We form a connection beyond words with our friend
as we open our heart and listen
What's Now?

Be fully present in every moment of life
For when you're lost in the wind
You miss the magic of what's right before your eyes

That magic forever exists in *What's Now*

Today's Happiness

we put in so much work
and stress out excessively
so we could
eventually
find a job that provides for us
and gives us the freedom
to experience happiness

how about
instead of viewing happiness as a future thing
we instill it every day in our lives?
if we lose sleep and tear ourselves apart now
for the purpose of having a "good job" and finding
happiness later...
we are doing ourselves a huge disservice

because today's happiness is just as important as tomorrow's

Society's Blueprint

throw away society's blueprint
you are not just another pawn in life's predictable
game
you are not just another number in the world's
population
you are not just another worker in a money churning
factory
you are a *human*
living out *your human experience*

so go make the absolute most of it

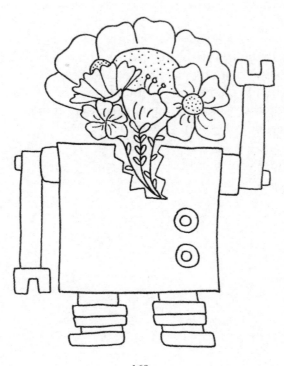

Mindset

i've always wondered
how some people could be so wealthy
seemingly have everything in life and more
and still feel so miserable inside
i've always wondered
how some people could have no home
barely make it by with scraps
and still smile as though life has granted them all the
gifts in the world

then i realized this...

the reality that you are living in is a work of your own
mind
the thoughts through which you perceive the world
dictate the reality through which you experience it
it doesn't matter what circumstances you're in
whether you are living in abundance
or whether you are living in close to nothing...
nothing doesn't mean *anything*

because your mind can create *anything* out of *nothing*

the moment you let go of all judgment is the same
moment your life becomes fully yours

You Will Rise

Dance freely. Laugh carelessly. Sing loudly. Walk boldly.

Life is far too precious to let the negative projections of others stifle who you are

You know who you are

You are a radiant being sharing joy and changing the world with just your smile
You are the rays of sun everyone craves after the clouds have been out for a while
You are a beautiful soul growing your wings and spreading Love throughout the day
You are the simple blessing people receive when they close their eyes and pray

Remain empowered in who you are even in the face of judgement

Sometimes, eyes that find the spirits living life in their full truth
Will turn to lips of discontent if they're intimidated by the view
Envy is the common culprit of a mouth with sour taste
Most can cure their discontent by putting more Love in their space

The negative energy people project onto you

Is a manifestation of the wound they carry within
themselves

So channel your expression in whatever way feels real
for you
Surround yourself with kind souls who show you love
for what you do
Allow your Highest Self to stand even among
captious eyes
Trust in who you know you are and from there...

You will rise

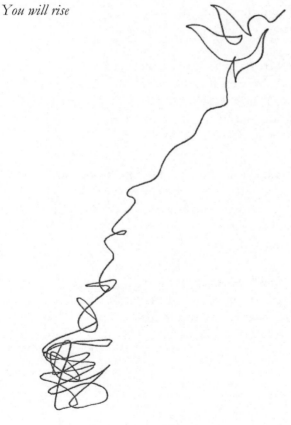

"Success"

One year from now, no one will ask
If you ended up with an A or B
What they'll want to know is how hard you try
How deeply you love
How big you dream

Five years from now, no one will know
If you were top among your class
What they'll observe is how you think
Through all the challenges
You surpass

Ten years from now, no one will care
If you went to Stanford or NYU
What they'll care about is the person you are
The attitude you bring
The goals you pursue

Twenty years from now, you'll reflect on life
And think about your high school years
What you'll remember is moments of laughter
Spontaneous nights
Adventures with peers

So if you're studying all day long
Don't stress so much about being the "best"
I promise you, having fun in life
Is much more of a "success"

who are you living for?

it might feel easier at times to shrink down so you
could live for other people's approval, but wow...

it is so much more liberating to expand into your
fullest power and live life for *you*

Curious Minds

Under the dim flicker of my bedside lamp
The textbooks are a jumble of formulas and facts
I find myself reciting the theorems
Soon to be forgotten artifacts

As the night drapes over me, I feel a magnetic
longing
To free myself into the unknown
I am submerged into a world of why's and how's
As the explorer breaks through my bones

I feel the urge to unleash the questions
That pulse wildly through my heart:
Why does Gabriel's Horn have finite volume?
How did chemists uncover Earth's intricate art?

Entranced by the why's and how's
A desire flows out from my center
To reach past the seat of an onlooker
And fill the seat of the inventor

So, I venture into the pathway of discovery…

This path is met with resistance
It's met with limiting beliefs
It's met with people who choose *cannot*
Rather than trusting in what *can be*

But curious minds innovate
They grasp every chance to explore
Even when faced with obstacles

Our open minds unlock closed doors

100 years ago, it would've been impossible
To sequence genomes and DNA
But now scientists work on studying
New genomes every day

See, the "impossible" is just a facade
A self-limiting belief that serves no good
When you free yourself into the why's and how's
Anything can be understood

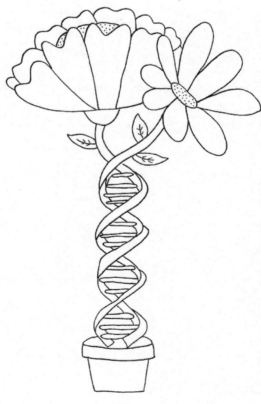

smile more and laugh often
you are creating a positive impact on this earth by
experiencing joy
the happiness you radiate is shared and amplified to
everyone around you
just by being happy, you are making a difference

Legacy

we talk so much about leaving an impact
about making our mark on this world
so our lives could outlive us
and we could be remembered
so many of us strive to do something big
to land in the textbook pages of a future generation
so we could feel like our existence mattered

for me?

leaving my mark means brightening someone's day
making just one person smile is enough
sharing my love and light everywhere I go
is the trail I'll leave of my existence

if i made even one human discover the bliss of being
alive
then my life served a purpose
we don't need to do something grand
for us to have a legacy...

i want to be remembered simply for my joy

Simple Blessings

simply because I have eyes that allow me to see the world in color

... I am happy

simply because I have hands that let me touch and feet that let me walk

... I am grateful

simply because I woke up this morning still breathing

... I am blessed

Happiness Is a Choice

today, I choose *happiness*

I choose to wake up and live life with love
I choose to see the beauty in all the simple things that
go unnoticed
I choose to smile at strangers and tell someone how
wonderful they are
I choose to go outside and soak in the sunshine
I choose to play with the earth and let my inner child
be free
I choose to smell the flowers and remind myself of
how much there is to be grateful for
I choose to hug my mama and tell my dad I love him
I choose to call my friends I haven't talked to in years
I choose to run with the wind and dance in the rain
because even the clouds can't dim the light I feel
within
I choose to watch the stars and find all my blessings
in the universe
I choose to go to sleep with a fuzzy feeling in my
heart because I know...

tomorrow, I get to choose happiness all over again

ACKNOWLEDGMENTS

Mom & Dad ~ For cheering me on since I first announced I wanted to be an author in 6th grade, all the way up until I published my first book at the end of college. I love you both for showing up in my life as my strongest support system. You mean the world to me.

Emmy Joy ~ For helping me discover my truth and lending me the eyes through which I found my purpose. The Light you radiate so brilliantly has ignited my own Light, and I am forever grateful to you for that. You are my biggest inspiration, truest friend, and best sister I could ever ask for.

Noah ~ For being my biggest fan and favorite muse. You are such a blessing in my life. Thank you for gifting me the most beautiful feeling in this world. You make writing love poems easy!

My soul tribe ~ When I met you all, my life transformed completely. You have taught me what true friendship means and inspired me to dream big. Our retreats together have catalyzed my love for life and the human experience. I wouldn't be who I am today if it wasn't for you all. I love you and I can't wait to see how beautifully our visions come together to change the world.

Mr. Conseur ~ My sixth-grade English teacher, the one who started this all. Thank you for teaching students in a way that inspires them to realize their full potential. The impact you made on me will carry through the rest of my life, as I continue to explore my creativity and share my writing. You are the teacher I will tell my kids about one day.

ABOUT THE AUTHOR

Neira was born and raised in San Diego, California. She is currently a university student at UCLA, studying Molecular Biology and minoring in Mathematical Biology. While she is on the path towards becoming a scientist, she has always felt inspired by the arts. When she was in 6th grade, her English teacher introduced a style of reformed learning, where creative expression had the freedom to flow. Since then, she has had ideas for many books, as she felt that being an author was part of her purpose. While she began and left some books unfinished, this poetry collection naturally emerged in parallel with her spiritual journey. For video content and live poetry read-alongs, follow her Instagram @neiraspoetry, where she shares more of her authentic expression.

Printed in Great Britain
by Amazon

22046332R00106